#KeriOn

By Dr. Keri Norris

Dedication

This work, as is all of my work, is inspired by the Sun and the Cub. Ashleon and Judah, you inspire me to greater heights and I love you like my next breath. You both are fearless and brave. I admire that, and on many days I am motivated by it.

It is my hope that in the same way you motivate me, this book and the lessons within will inspire others to do more than live- to THRIVE. Remember, whatever life brings your way, choose JOY and #KeriOn.

Introduction

You matter. You have a voice, you are valued, and you are loved. Those are all true, whether you realize it or not. This book was born out of a painful time in my life,when I had NO choice but to forge ahead and #KeriOn. God left me to find the positive and the lessons in the midst of loss, confusion, and illness that were wreaking havoc on my body.

Often in life, we read meaningful quotes or bask in mantras left by great writers such as Maya Angelou, Anais Nin, or Audrey Lorde. Some find their inspiration and mantras in religious texts like the Qur'an, the Bible, or the Torah. I have found my inspiration somewhere in between those authors and those religious texts, but what has changed my life most are lessons learned from painful moments that I *believed* I couldn't get through. I've been mostly inspired by my own quips and thoughts during very dark times, and how I have pulled on my innate resilience to #KeriOn. I am often asked how I have survived "intact" with all that I have been through, and I often answer, "Grace". However, I also attribute it to having a healthy sense of humor, being loved by my family, and being okay with being uncomfortable sometimes.

I started this journey in late 2015, after losing two very important men in my life and I felt as if I was constantly losing everything around me- but I had to push on. I have always liked play on words and phrases, so I began hash tagging my given first name as a play on the words carry on. #KeriOn was born out of encouraging myself, my social media friends and family, and anyone who so happened to read my updates. It is important to #KeriOn in life and to know that regardless of what is going on with me, I am always "ON". I also secretly play with the fact that life happens, and there have been times where I was almost K-O'ed- but I am still standing. And so are you!

So because I love you and you are valued, I decided to share a 52-week journey of uplifting insight and lessons for you to walk through. It is my purpose and pleasure to help you find the light in your life and #KeriOn.

Table of Contents

Week One

> *Distractions will keep you from the promise.*
> *FOCUS. #KeriOn*

In life we are oftentimes faced with opportunities to grow that may be painful. There is so much purpose in this pain and we have to stay the course in order to grow and move to the next level that will propel us to greater heights. During these times of change -where we are faced with our most important decisions- we become distracted by people, situations and oppositions that aren't new.

Have you ever asked yourself, "Why does this person keep appearing in my life?" It is because you have failed the test time and time again of learning to push past problems, and instead focus on the outcome to be able to improve in life. An ex, a problem family member or a challenging co-worker - all of these are distractions from your purpose. Once you recognize this, you are then empowered to ignore, focus and #KeriOn. Pass the test to get to what is promised to you and what is exclusively meant for you. Learn to get "unstuck" and stop focusing on others; they are deliberate distractions for a reason. For instance, problem family members cannot be healed by your efforts or attention. That ex is an ex for a reason, and they haven't changed. Your challenging co-worker desires to keep you from reaching greater heights and is purposely there to distract you.

This week, your challenge is to list out those persons or situations that always "knock you off your game," so that you easily recognize the distractions when they come. If you name a thing and give a face to it, then you can recognize and address it accordingly when faced with it again. Think of the things that keep you in good spirits- laughing, smiling, upbeat- and surround yourself with those things. Again, give NO energy to the person or situation that is negative.

Should you verbally say the words"you are a distraction" to anyone? No. What is understood does not need to be explained; all you need to do is STOP participating and simply #KeriOn.

WEEKLY ASSIGNMENT:

Day 1: List those persons and situations that distract you

Day 2: List the current opportunities that you have in front of you

Day 3: What positive things help you to focus on your goals? Do one of them today.

Day 4: If you allow distractions to win, what do you lose?

Day 5: When you focus, what do you gain?

Week Two

We often appear to stand strong and make bold statements. Sometimes we're still permissive and beg of acceptance.#KeriOn

I have some associates who post some of the most positive and empowering posts ever on social media, and who make statements in conversation as if they have it all figured out. No one is perfect, no one has it all figured out. Some people create these lives, personas, and statements to encourage themselves, while others just are trying to convince you that they truly have it all together.

It is my experience that the most confident person of all has areas where they are begging for acceptance. We are so easily distracted by bravado, accomplishments, titles, and material things that we do not pay attention to over-compensation and the need to always announce WHO you are to the world. You may have the title of boss in your place of business, but you are a peasant in the world and in life. You beg for acceptance, and your bold statements are actually permissions to be you. Let that sink in.

There is nothing wrong with self-awareness, knowing who you are, and standing in your power. The issue comes in when you always have to announce or explain it. Think about the one friend you know who always states how independent they are,who gives long speeches on how they have arrived, and then ends the sentence in "right"? Why does he or she require permission from you to be who they are, or for you to be the audience to their power? Don't be that lame person- be you. I encourage you to be strong and make strides,however I am known for always saying "Let your work speak for you". You don't have to run your mouth or get "Amens" in order to feel as if you are on the right path and doing the right things.

This week your task is to work on standing in your power without the need for approvals.

WEEKLY ASSIGNMENT:

Day 1: Describe yourself in a paragraph or a list. WARNING: Be honest about who you are RIGHT NOW.

Day 2: List out your insecurities and areas where you may feel inadequate.

Day 3: What are your strengths? Practice one of them today.

Day 4: What if you never achieve acceptance or praise from others. What will you lose?

Day 5: When you love yourself right where you are without applause from others, what do you gain?

Week Three

This lesson is the one I had the hardest time learning. I spent so much of my own time going in circles about how the person who hurt me had caused tremendous pain, which was lingering. I also spent a great amount of time trying to figure out why the suffering was so long and all consuming. What a fool! I can laugh at myself now.

I had to learn to choose pain. Yes, I said choose pain. If something cuts or injures you, there is an immediate sting, hurt, or ouch. Let. That. Be. It. In other words, treat the injury and move on. Don't nurse your pain, mull over it, and keep checking on it to see how it heals. Treat it and let it heal naturally. This is how you eliminate suffering. Suffering is self-inflicted because you won't let go and #KeriOn. Choose pain and let that be it.

I'm going to share a personal lesson with you about a time when I set myself up for hurt. I entered into a relationship with a guy who I knew I had NO future with whatsoever; however, I adored him and loved the time we spent together. The inevitable pain showed up when he was no longer interested in continuing on in a relationship of any kind with me,and I decided to suffer by not letting go and healing from it. I decided to suffer when I would still reach out and say"Hello", "How are you?", or "Happy Birthday" to a man who wanted nothing more to do with me. I was causing my own suffering by trying to figure out where I went wrong. Well dummy (talking to myself), you knew from jump what it was and what it would never be- yet you put your hope in a thing you knew was a dead end,and chose to suffer unnecessarily.

This week's lesson will be hard. But I believe in you. You picked up this book because you are ready to heal and to live your best life. So let's #KeriOn

WEEKLY ASSIGNMENT:

Day 1: List the top ten things that pain ycu - emotionally, physically, spiritually.

Day 2: List the ways in which you have suffered as a result of each of those 10 things.

Day 3: What keeps you from feeling the pain and falling into suffering? Do that activity today.

Day 4: If you allow suffering to take over your life, what do you lose?

Day 5: When you feel the pain but CHOOSE not to suffer, what do you gain?

Week Four

Your soul mate just might be ugly.#KeriOn

We have these grandiose ideas of what our soul mate looks like, acts like, earns, and how they show us love. Let go of it now! Throw the entire list away. Throw the entire fantasy away. I will tell you now that love, real love, looks nothing like you imagined. What if I told you that love is scrawny, has no credit, wears a Jheri curl, and drives a beat-up Pinto? You would call me crazy. (By the way, it doesn't…I am just making a point here.)

But think of this- love will never be all the fantasies combined that you picture in your mind. If you model it after your father, there's only one of him. If you model it after your mother, there's only one of her. Let's be clear. Focus on the character of who you want, not what she or he looks like, because looks fade. Your soul mate is nothing like you imagined, at all-the packaging, the job, or the voice. I have been in love with Morris Chestnut for years, but that's somebody else's soul mate- not mine. And quite frankly, he may not be all that I imagine he is (although I doubt it, but I digress). What is meant for you, is meant for you, so #KeriOn.

Whatever or whoever you believe in, believe in this... whoever you are truly meant to be with will manifest as soon as you let go of that list and your expectations. In order to receive love, you must BE LOVE. This week's lesson will revisit your concept of soul mate and love.

WEEKLY ASSIGNMENT:

Day 1: List the characteristics that you want in the perfect soul mate. Say out loud, "forgive me." Burn the list.

Day 2: List all of your characteristics and be HONEST about who you are - good and bad.

Day 3: What activities make you feel loved? Do one of them today.

Day 4: If you attract someone who mirrors who you are RIGHT NOW, what do you gain?

Day 5: What areas should you work on in order to be a good soul mate?

Week Five

Learn to rejoice with others, forgive, and ask for forgiveness. Perhaps you will unlock a door for yourself.#KeriOn

It is when we can rejoice with others and celebrate them that we open doors of blessings for ourselves. I am a believer that there is room for everyone to succeed. The definition of success varies from person to person; however, feeling a sense of fulfillment and accomplishment is important to everyone. Learn to celebrate with others, even if you are going through a rough time. Don't rain on your friend, family, or associate's parade. REJOICE WITH THEM.

Forgive yourself for the wrongs you have done to others, but most importantly, forgive yourself for the wrongs you have committed against yourself. One of the hardest things I have had to do was to forgive myself. I have beat myself up much more than others have, and I had to forgive my mistakes and my choice to suffer. I had to learn that forgiveness isn't only about others, it's about self also. I also learned that once I forgave someone, myself included, there seemed to be new opportunities or rewards right around the corner.

Forgive everybody for everything. Let me say that again. Forgive everybody. For everything. I have been through some unimaginable shit in my lifetime, but there is not one person in my life, past or present,that does not have my forgiveness. Forgiveness truly frees you to be able to #KeriOn and get to the happy life you deserve. Who has time to be worn down by the things of the past? Abused or neglected? Forgive. Cheated on? Forgive. Your boss is an idiot with power? Forgive. Friends betrayed you? Forgive. Family hurt you? Forgive. Someone hurt your loved one? Forgive. There is such power in forgiveness and there is freedom in it as well.

This week's lesson will focus on rejoicing with others and forgiveness.

WEEKLY ASSIGNMENT:

Day 1: List those persons that you need to forgive (go as far back as you can remember).

Day 2: List the things that you must forgive yourself for.

Day 3: What things make you feel free? Do one of them today.

Day 4: If you allow unforgiveness or jealousy to rule your life, what do you lose?

Day 5: When you forgive yourself and others, what do you gain?

— ❧ —

Week Six

If no one else has told you today...you are beautiful, you are amazing, you are loved.
#KeriOn

Self-affirmations are amazing. Everyone does not have close family or friends, but we all can use some encouragement to #KeriOn. Viewing yourself in a positive, yet humble light does wonders for your spirit and draws more positivity from others. Things happen in life, but a positive word, compliment,or affirmation goes a long way, especially if you practice it in the morning.

Learn to compliment others and in return you will see that they will do the same. I don't know you, but I love you; if I didn't, I would not have written this book to try and get you to #KeriOn to live your best and most fulfilling life. You should embody the positive affirmations that speak to you the most. Find quotes from songs, poems, or famous persons that inspire you and make you feel great about yourself and place them throughout your home to remind you of your greatness. I once had a guy that I dated say, "I love your quotes that are everywhere and the one on the fridge is my favorite." He was inspired and knows that I love myself, which in turn set a standard for him and his respect for me.

Don't live for affirmations from others; if you get them, great, but if you do not, that is fine too. You don't want to regress,asking permissions, and seeking validation again (reminder, that's for parking. not self-love). I want you to work towards a sense of higher self and self-worth. You are the best person ever and no one has your gifts, nor can they be you. Remember to be confident, not arrogant.

This week's lesson focuses on getting to the core of your self evaluation and self-love.

WEEKLY ASSIGNMENT:

Day 1: List those characteristics that are positive about you - place quotes around the house that reflect these characteristics.

Day 2: List the positive things that other say about you.

Day 3: What things make you feel valued? Do one of them today.

Day 4: If you focus on the negative things, what do you lose?

Day 5: When you practice daily affirmations, what do you gain?

Week Seven

THE most sacred space in this world, women OWN and were born with...protect that! Once you OWN THAT, you'll know your worth and won't settle. #KeriOn

---

Women are the givers of life, and that is a powerful gift; the womb is a sacred space. Whether a woman chooses to become a mother or not, she still possesses the gift of being able to choose. Whomever she loves values that gift and her sacred space- or at least they should. If you find that you are not being valued and held in the highest regard, check yourself - QUICKLY.

Many times, we may find ourselves in unhealthy attachments and we must reevaluate these connections as we were not created to be misused or abused. Nor were we created to misuse or abuse our sacred spaces. As in other chapters, forgive yourself for past transgressions against yourself and #KeriOn. Most importantly, STOP THAT SHIT and don't do it again. Protect yourself, know your worth, and hold onto your sacred space until you know that you know you are valued and protected. Transference of disease is not the only thing you should be concerned about; concern yourself with transference of dis-ease. Soul ties are hard to break- but you CAN break them.

This week's lesson focuses on owning and valuing your sacred space.

WEEKLY ASSIGNMENT:

Day 1: List unhealthy relationships that you have had or are engaging in. Forgive them and forgive yourself.

Day 2: Center yourself with prayer, Reiki, or meditation each morning to remind you of your value.

Day 3: Vtox or work with a Reiki master to realign your sacral chakra. Do one of them today.

Day 4: If you allow misuse and abuse to continue, what do you lose?

Day 5: When you value yourself, what do you gain?

Week Eight

You commit to what you value. If you value yourself then others must also. How you treat you is how they will treat you. Be the love that you want in return, and when you do not see your return on investment (ROI), withdraw, and #KeriOn, quickly. Cut all ties and keep it pushing.

I once dated someone, and he was amazing, attentive, and loving- then things changed. I don't know why people assume you can't see or detect a change in their habits. You have to maintain the exact same time, attention, and activities that you used to get a person to keep them. It's truly that simple. When the calls start lagging, and you start canceling or rescheduling outings, there is a problem. When you move from calls and Face Time to text only, MAYDAY! You are in trouble and you need to go ahead fire the person. It's just like a job. If you don't call or don't show, it's pink slip time.

Know when it cannot be salvaged. Know when you can't fix a thing. Know your value and value your time.

This week's lesson is to learn when to fire someone and #KeriOn.

WEEKLY ASSIGNMENT:

Day 1: List the things you enjoyed doing with your partner in the beginning.

Day 2: List how things have changed since that time (don't include kids or illness).

Day 3: What things make you feel wanted by your partner? Do one of them today with your partner.

Day 4: If you allow neglect and emotional abuse, what do you lose?

Day 5: When you value yourself, what do you gain?

Week Nine

2015 was the year from HELL for me, but there were so many lessons that I learned. Loss is painful and indescribable (at least for me). I had many health challenges in 2015, and doctors were trying to figure out the mysterious illness that I had which was getting worse by the day. My father died, and six months later my heart, a man I loved like no other, died as well. I was devastated. But I had to find it within me to #KeriOn.

Sometimes in loss, you have to stop and think about what you gained through that loss. My Dad was not perfect, but he was mine. He was brutally critical and honest, but he laced it with humor and love for his kids. My sisters and I are grateful for the time we had with him and each year we celebrate him. But during the loss, I realized how many people don't have a Dad or an example of what a man should be or should do. My father, if nothing else, was a provider and a teacher. He never missed one graduation for me or one special performance. To me, he was a King- flawed, but a King. Many of the characteristics that I am complimented on are things I learned from my Dad.

The love of my life, Kings (his actual name), loved me in a way I was not used to and was resistant to in the beginning. He too was brutally honest with me and laced his truth with love and humor. He would say things like "Finally, I realize there IS something you can't do – sing," or "You really need to get out of your own way." I was so injured when he found me that I could not appreciate what I had, and I drove a wedge in between us. After we broke up, I realized that I had experienced real love as it should be, and I am fortunate to be able to say that. But when he died, I felt my soul cry out, and I couldn't breathe until God patted me on the back like a newborn baby and forced me to take a breath.

The loss almost consumed me, but I had to #KeriOn. This week's lesson is about finding the good in the loss and moving forward in purpose.

WEEKLY ASSIGNMENT:

Day 1: List the losses that have affected you the most.

Day 2: List the lessons or blessings attached to all of those losses.

Day 3: What things make you feel alive and grateful? Do one of them today.

Day 4: If you allow yourself to wallow in what you lost, what else do you lose?

Day 5: When you find the blessings and your passion, what do you gain?

※

Week Ten

Sometimes you have to close the door. LOCK IT. Wall slide. Have the ugly cry. Get up again and dust yourself off, then make it all beautiful. AGAIN. #KeriOn

I have endured some ungodly betrayals in my lifetime. Friends, family, lovers, '"Was band", and colleagues have betrayed me in ways that you cannot imagine. I used to always say, 'You can't write this', but here I am, writing it. The important lessons associated with betrayal, are to keep your guard up like a boxer and know that whomever you trust or confide in has the ability to betray you with your most vulnerable things.

When betrayal takes place, forgive, and #KeriOn. Do not keep these people in your life. We often think that forgiveness entitles a person to stay in our lives- NO.

Forgive the person and be cordial in the streets but I say NO SECOND CHANCES to be in my intimate environment or setting. Close the door on that relationship, lock it, grieve the relationship, and give it a proper 15 minutes of fame, then #KeriOn. We do not invest time and energy into things that no longer serve us in a positive manner. Let it go. Let them go.

The lesson this week focuses on naming the betrayal, grieving the relationship and moving on.

WEEKLY ASSIGNMENT:

Day 1: List those persons that betrayed you and how. Then,burn the paper and release it into the wind.

Day 2: List how you contributed to your own betrayal (Do you trust too easily or talk too much?)

Day 3: What things make you feel beautiful and valued? Do one of them today.

Day 4: If you allow betrayals to consume you, what do you lose?

Day 5: When you forgive yourself and others, what do you gain?

Your experiences, choices, and life will show you the difference between those who are your friends versus those who are your associates. #KeriOn

Have you ever been out somewhere and people are trying to connect with you, so they will ask a laundry list of questions? I despise that. Small talk isn't my forte. But one of the things that happens is that people will inquire about other people. Here is where you need to pay close attention, because I am going to school you on how to answer the questions.

When approached about another person, consider that person's motive. Are they genuinely trying to connect with you, gain information about someone, or repeat whatever you said about that person? Either way, know that your answer can become public domain.

When asked, "Do you know Sally Sue?," your answer should be honest and short. It will save you a headache in the long run. You can answer this in one of three ways: No, I don't know her, or Yes, I know OF her, or Yes, I know her. There is a huge difference between knowing someone and knowing of them. If you cannot name their closest relative, their significant other, or you haven't been to their Mama's house - you do not know them, you know of them (this includes having worked with them in the past). Be honest and don't try and extrapolate bits and pieces of information that you think you know in order to pretend to know the person. Associates, Acquaintances, Friends, and Coworkers are different words and should not be used interchangeably. This also comes into play when you are going through a serious event. Friends show up no matter what. Pay attention to who shows up, and then #KeriOn.

The lesson this week focuses on the differences between friends and people you know.

WEEKLY ASSIGNMENT:

Day 1: List those people who show up for you in bad times and who celebrate you in good times.

Day 2: Be honest about who you know and who you know of.

Day 3: What things do you value with friends? Do one of them today with a true friend.

Day 4: If you allow everyone in your circle, what do you lose?

Day 5: When you hold on to valued and proven friends, what do you gain?

Week Twelve

Validation is for parking. Do your best to stay professional and a great example within your circle of influence; however, do not spend time worrying about what others think of you. What others think of you is NONE of your business. In a world of social media where some people look for likes, laughs, and attention, be the real. Be you and be respectful, but stand your ground and don't fret over who told whom to go and look at what you just posted.

Let's be honest- there is a such thing as netiquette, and you should be cognizant about your online associations and future business opportunities - but BE YOU. If you know that your thoughts and posts are wild, perhaps your page should be private, and you shouldn't friend coworkers, socialites, or the like. I am well aware that the same associate that pointed out someone else's beach pictures is the exact same one drawing attention to other people's controversial posts, including mine. But if you live to please everyone, you will drive yourself insane. Delete the messy folks out of your life and reset so that you can #KeriOn. Here are my rules: if it affects your money - don't say it or post it. If it doesn't, do you!

This week's lesson is about freedom from needing validation.

WEEKLY ASSIGNMENT:

Day 1: List the things that you value most.

Day 2: List the things that you have done, said, or participated in that may negatively impact what you value.

Day 3: What things make you feel free? Do one of them today.

Day 4: If you allow needing validation to rule you, what do you lose?

Day 5: When you are true to who you are, what do you gain?

Week Thirteen

In a time when there are so many articles on the difficulty of marriages and having a relationship, especially for women of color, you have to value when a woman is interested in you. With all these "independent" women out here, there is quite a ruckus in social settings which is disrupting the balance in love and dating. In heterosexual relationships, some say that the roles have been reversed because women are out here doing it for themselves and are breadwinners. If a woman does not need you financially, don't sweat it because she wants you. She just doesn't need you in that way. So get over it, and #KeriOn.

When a woman decides that she is interested, she commits to that interest. Don't take it for granted, because she doesn't need you how you want to be needed. And women won't use your financial status to try and lead or manipulate you. But let me be clear, if you start slacking and she is unaffected, it is because she doesn't miss your presence, and you are showing her that she is okay without you. We see so many women who refer to themselves as King; hell there are some who refer to Beyoncé as King B, but I guarantee there is balance there and her counterpart knows that she knows how to #KeriOn if she so desires.

The lesson this week is to focus on being fine with being wanted and not needed.

WEEKLY ASSIGNMENT:

Day 1: List why you feel like it's more important to be needed versus wanted.

Day 2: List the things that your significant other does to show that you are wanted.

Day 3: What things make you feel wanted? Do one of them today.

Day 4: If you allow dependence to rule, what do you lose?

Day 5: When you are loved without condition, what do you gain?

Week Fourteen

*Who is on the board of directors in your life?
Think about the top 5 people you spend time
with. How are they directing your life? Review
your circle and decide if you need a new board.
#KeriOn.*

Be clear, I am not saying to go out and get a bunch of "yes" people because that is equally dangerous.

We spend time with people who are close to us, yet never think about their influence on our thinking and our actions. The people you spend the most time with enhance your choices and decisions. You tend to share with them your accolades, your disappointments, and your dreams. They can build or break them. I always tell people do not take advice from anyone you aren't willing to trade places with. Why would you take career advice from someone who hasn't had a stable job in years? Why would you take advice on your marriage from a single person who has never been married,nor had a successful relationship?

Your board of directors are those you spend the most time with and those who counsel you. Review your circle, replace some members if need be, and learn to #KeriOn without explanation. Some people will hang on to you because of where you are going and hope that they will come along. Some people hang on just to see what you are doing and to secretly compete. YOU are your biggest competition. Focus on your own race.

This week's lesson is to focus on your board of directors.

WEEKLY ASSIGNMENT:

Day 1: List the five people you spend the most time with.

Day 2: List the things that you gain from those 5 people; are they always positive?

Day 3: Which person is most encouraging and positive? Do something with that person today.

Day 4: If your board is mainly negative, what do you lose?

Day 5: When you choose positive and supportive board members, what do you gain?

Week Fifteen

The majority of law suits, messy divorces, arguments, and misunderstandings are based on bad communication. Leave no room for interpretation- be transparent, be honest, and if you say it once you better be woman or man enough to say it again (Thanks Dad for that advice). There is a difference between being rude and crass versus being truthful and transparent.

In business and in love, transparency is what keeps communications and success at the forefront. Ever notice how a couple who is dating gets confused on what they are to one another? That's because someone wasn't absolutely clear about the definitions and parameters of the agreement. Be blunt.

And when a person tells you who they are, believe them. Also, when a person tells you what they do and don't want, never believe that you are the one who can change their mind; that's fool's gold. Be clear, let them roll you up and take a hit, then #KeriOn. There is no guess work or confusion later, and it saves time and headaches.

The lesson this week is to recognize where you need to be blunt.

WEEKLY ASSIGNMENT:

Day 1: List those areas where you have not been blunt with people.

Day 2: List the ways in which you can have transparent communication with others.

Day 3: What things make you feel valued? Do one of them today.

Day 4: If you allow miscommunication or half-truths, what do you lose?

Day 5: When you express your honest viewpoint, what do you gain?

Week Sixteen

Be so dope, he wants to roll you up and take a hit. Be addictive.#KeriOn

In dating, whomever you are interested in should be enamored with how wonderful you are. You are the hottest thing going- and you better know it! You must be in tune with what is happening with you both so that you both are each other's peace and place of rest. If work or the world is difficult, no one wants to come home to hear complaining or questioning about trivial things without solutions. Be solution-based. Be a comfort. Be supportive within reason.

Be dope. Show your significant other why you love them, and why they should always be in love with you. Trouble will come, it is inevitable; but it's all in HOW you handle it. Prioritize the issues, and address them one by one together. Be a problem solver. Positivity gets you where looks can't keep you (we know that fades). Remember ladies, your boyfriend is not your good girlfriend. Once you learn this, you can #KeriOn.

This week's lesson addresses how and where we focus our energies.

WEEKLY ASSIGNMENT:

Day 1: List the ways in which your significant other thinks that you are dope (and reflect on their compliments. Be sure to refrain from sharing your personal opinion here.

Day 2: List the ways in which you can be more positive.

Day 3: What things make you feel in tune with your partner? Do one of them today.

Day 4: If you allow complaining and fighting to rule your relationship, what do you lose?

Day 5: When you communicate in positive ways, what do you gain?

Week Seventeen

Count it all joy that you have an earthly or heavenly mother that was positive and loving; everyone can't say that. #KeriOn

Oftentimes we take for granted that all families don't look the same, and that we do not have the same experiences growing up. I once had a friend to approach me about an important project she was working on with fatherless daughters, which I fully supported, but she assumed that I had grown up without my Dad. My Dad has always been present and a strong influence in my life. Some women do not have positive relationships with their Mom, so it is hard for them to relate to those who say that their Mom is their best friend. Some people are raised by grandparents, extended family members, or complete strangers.

If you are fortunate enough to have had a positive Mother/Father figure in your life, count it all joy! So many of the problems we see in society today are directly related to the absence of one or more positive examples of parenthood. Don't feel bad or counted out if you didn't have positive and loving parents. What counts is how you heal and move forward. #KeriOn

This week's lesson focuses on learning how to grieve what you didn't have, and move on.

WEEKLY ASSIGNMENT:

Day 1: List the positive experiences that you had with your Mother/Father figure.

Day 2: List the things that you must forgive of your Mother/Father figure.

Day 3: What things make you feel loved? Do one of them today.

Day 4: If you allow wallowing in pity or unforgiveness, what do you lose?

Day 5: When you focus on being better for the future, what do you gain?

Week Eighteen

To see the joy on the face of others is great...to know joy for oneself is a gift.#KeriOn

Learn to celebrate with others and stop living a life of comparison. When we celebrate with others, we are open to experience joy of our own. Sit on the front row and clap for others, applaud them in their successes, and do it with sincerity. I always refer to this as overflow. Celebrate with others and you will reap the overflow of joy by knowing how to be happy for others.

I had a friend who I would share many of my ups and downs with. She was always all ears when I was going through something dramatic, but when things were good or awesome for me, her response would be "That is so great." It was dry as hell. Not very celebratory or convincing. Pay attention to those who sit in your front row but don't clap. They are there for a front seat to your challenges and downfalls, but not to cheer you on in victories. Be sure to be a better friend and supporter to others and #KeriOn.

The lesson this week is to recognize joy for others and find joy for yourself.

WEEKLY ASSIGNMENT:

Day 1: List those persons that celebrate you and your accomplishments- who do you cheer for?

Day 2: List those persons that seem lackluster and half supportive in your life.

Day 3: What things make you feel celebrated? Do one of them today.

Day 4: If you allow false friends in your inner circles, what do you lose?

Day 5: When you celebrate with others, what do you gain?

✦

Week Nineteen

Refuse to walk in bitterness, anger, or defeat.
Choose LIFE. Choose wisely. Step out on faith
and trust that it all works out. #KeriOn

Man, listen...life can be tricky and sometimes trying. Step out on faith and #KeriOn. If you walked around keeping count of all the wrongs done to you, where is the room for joy and the good in life? We all experience setbacks, hardships and disappointments; however, you can't wallow in it or mope in self-pity. Well you can, but you shouldn't stay in a place of 'woe is me'. As things happen, process the situation, and heal and move on.

Smiling and finding the joy in all things allows us to move past hurts. Walking by faith allows us to dream for the future and put our hope in better days ahead. There are too many people in this world walking around in anger and bitterness; they are emotionally and spiritually dead. Choose life. I dare you.

This week's lesson is to move past anger and defeat and to LIVE.

WEEKLY ASSIGNMENT:

Day 1: List those instances where faith anchored you through a hard time.

Day 2: List the things that you have allowed to feel defeated.

Day 3: What positive things make you feel alive? Do one of them today.

Day 4: If you allow bitterness to rule your life, what do you lose?

Day 5: When you have faith and choose life, what do you gain?

Week Twenty

You do realize that people don't only troll social media. They troll your life. #KeriOn

Trolls have become more popular on social media because of the controversy and "messiness" they stir up when they post or get involved in an exchange. Well, trolls exist in everyday life. Trolls are your messy family members, associates, or coworkers who keep up strife because peace is just too bland for them. These people operate in chaos and dysfunction because they enjoy drama. Disconnect and #KeriOn.

I had a co-worker who would go around pretending to know things and trying to fish information out of everyone so that she could create strife. She never had conversations with everyone present, but cowardly would talk to everyone separately and create major drama and chaos.

She fed off of it and enjoyed when people were not getting along because as long as people were focused on the drama, no one could focus on her flaws. Trolls can be in person and not just online. The deal is to just leave them to their own antics and #KeriOn. Eventually, everyone catches on to the game, no one participates, and the troll is left alone to their own demise and self-hate.

This week's lesson is to recognize the trolls in your life and actively disengage them.

WEEKLY ASSIGNMENT:

Day 1: List those persons that you recognize as trolls (yourself included if it applies).

Day 2: List the things that you must ignore if you are dealing with a troll.

Day 3: What things make you feel positive? Do one of them today.

Day 4: If you allow trolls and their drama to rule your life, what do you lose?

Day 5: When you give no place to trolls, what do you gain?

Week Twenty-One

When a person has wronged you in some way, revenge is never the answer. Whether you believe in Karma, reaping and sowing, or the law of attraction, trust and believe that whatever you put out comes back full force. Sometimes karma is quick and other times it is delayed; however it plays out, don't sit and wait to see it. #KeriOn.

If I don't believe anything else, I believe that whatever you sow in the light or dark will come back to you full force. I try to be very careful of how I treat others, mindful of what I entertain, and what I am involved in - I suggest that everyone think before they act in anyway. As I have told several of my friends, be very careful with being out here without a care in the world because sometimes when harvest comes, it doesn't come to you, it hits your kids. I love my Sun and his family enough to sow good, that they might see some grace in their own lives.

This week's lesson is to focus on moving on quickly from wrong doings, and allowing Karma to run its course.

WEEKLY ASSIGNMENT:

Day 1: List those instances where you have sowed negative things.

Day 2: List those instances where you have sowed positive things.

Day 3: What things make you feel like grace is operating in your life? Do one of them today.

Day 4: If you hang on to things of the past, what do you lose?

Day 5: When you always act in kindness, what do you gain?

Week Twenty Two

Self care isn't selfish. #KeriOn

People will try and make you feel guilty for not attending their outings and events, not knowing all that you are doing with your magnificent life, or not knowing that you are dealing with some ailment that keeps you from attending events. Forget them and #KeriOn. If you dog your body out and die, they will send a card, bring chicken or ham to your family, be sad for a day, and move on. Take care of yourself and listen to your body.

There are times I will accept an invitation with the full intention of showing up, but I am tired or just cannot make it. When your body or your mind tells you that you need rest, LISTEN. Self-care is not selfish and anyone who says anything different should not be in your circle.

You must pay attention to your body because there is only ONE you and you are valuable, needed, and appreciated. So, rest yourself.

This week's lesson is to listen to your inner voice when it comes to rest and relaxation.

WEEKLY ASSIGNMENT:

Day 1: List your cues for when you need to practice self-care.

Day 2: List the things that you enjoy doing for self-care.

Day 3: What things make you feel relaxed? Do one of them today.

Day 4: If you allow other people's schedules and demands to rule you, what do you lose?

Day 5: When you practice self-care, what do you gain?

Week Twenty-Three

Life throws curves and hits hard...be a short stop.#KeriOn

Expect the unexpected. Life is a beautiful and complex journey with an unknown destination. STAY READY. There will be curves, twists, and turns throughout your life, but it's all in how you handle it. Life will sometimes hit you hard; wear your protective gear (whatever keeps you centered), and #KeriOn.

When the unexpected happens, do your very best not to fall apart. Breathe, focus, keep your eyes on God, and put your mitt on to catch whatever is being thrown at you. Be a short stop. Be flexible. Be limber. Be quick. If you linger too long, you will surely lose and cost yourself and your team (family, coworkers, and friends).

This week's lesson is about being ready and staying ready for the unexpected. Do not live in fear or anxiety, but be prepared.

WEEKLY ASSIGNMENT:

Day 1: List some of those unexpected things that have happened in the past.

Day 2: List the best and most positive responses that you have had to life's curve balls.

Day 3: What things make you feel prepared and productive? Do one of them today.

Day 4: If you allow life's curves to run you around, what do you lose?

Day 5: When you stay ready (prayer, meditation, positive outlook), what do you gain?

Week Twenty Four

There is NO more time. Love today. Live today. Laugh today. Forgive. Love. Laugh. Eat more bacon. Drink more wine. #KeriOn

---

I remember a conversation in high school when an associate stated, "When I get older, I am going to be one of those saved, sold out older ladies." This young lady was counting on being here in her older years; she assumed that she would live forever. The time to live is now. The time to love is now. Eat more bacon. Drink more wine and #KeriOn.

I love, love, love bacon. Did I say I love bacon? It is the one thing that challenges my pescatarian lifestyle. I enjoy a nice smooth wine with great conversation after a long day of mentally challenging work. These are the small rewards that I give myself along the way because I do not assume that I have more time to live, to love, and to enjoy. Time is short, and life is even shorter. I was just a new mom, and now my baby is almost 29. Time flies.

The lesson this week is, it's good to plan for the future, but LIVE along the way.

WEEKLY ASSIGNMENT:

Day 1: List out the things you want to do that make you happy.

Day 2: Make your bucket list and check things off each week.

Day 3: What things make you feel ALIVE? Do one of them today.

Day 4: If you focus on the future more than the present, what do you lose?

Day 5: When you allow yourself to truly LIVE, what do you gain?

✺

Week Twenty Five

*Don't give up your joy, peace, or hope for anyone.
If you have to second guess it, walk away. Life is
short. #KeriOn*

You have no more time, so why waste it proving your worth to those who have made up their mind about who you are? Quit chasing people, trying to tell them who you are and how they should value you. If you are the only friend making all the effort, or you feel like you are in a relationship alone - STOP IT. If you have to second guess it, walk away, and #KeriOn.

We give so much of ourselves and our time to others in hopes that they will see our value and love us unconditionally in return. Hear me good. Once they have made up their minds about who you are, you cannot change their mind. You cannot love, gift, smooch, or weasel your way into a different spot in people's lives. If you have to second guess it, walk away and be content in prioritizing yourself. Hold those in high regard who do the same for you.

This week's lesson is about staying in reciprocal alliances/relationships.

WEEKLY ASSIGNMENT:

Day 1: List those relationships that are truly reciprocal.

Day 2: List those relationships that make you self-doubt or make you feel as if you are chasing the person.

Day 3: What things make you feel appreciated? Do one of them today.

Day 4: If you allow yourself to be an option, what do you lose?

Day 5: When you are in fully reciprocal relationships, what do you gain?

Week Twenty Six

To go from exceptional to average is not
acceptable.#KeriOn

Never dim your light so that others can feel better about themselves, which is a disservice to you and them. If you are exceptional, which I am sure that you are, stay true to yourself and shine! If you try to blend in with average people who aspire to do nothing more, then you will lose yourself and become average. Never, ever esteem yourself in higher regard than your fellow man but do keep company with those who push you to be your best self.

To go backwards is against the grain, and to surround yourself with people who take issue with you being exceptional works against you. If people shrink when they are in your light or greatness, that's on them- not on you. Who are you to shy away from your blessed talents and God-given gifts to make others feel better about themselves? Don't do it. Keep shining and #KeriOn.

This week's lesson is about letting your light shine.

WEEKLY ASSIGNMENT:

Day 1: List the gifts and talents that you are proud of.

Day 2: List the ways in which you can highlight your talents and gifts.

Day 3: What things make you feel useful? Do one of them today.

Day 4: If you dim your light, what do you lose?

Day 5: When you allow your light to shine, what do you gain?

Week Twenty Seven

Love your skin....and your accent. You are an acquired taste. #KeriOn

Everyone doesn't look like you, and that's a good thing. Just make sure that you love you! We all have problem areas that we don't like about ourselves. If you have one, work on it! But don't ever place your value on what others say about your appearance or their preference. In and out of our culture, there are critiques about hair, skin color, shape, fitness, etc., but as long as you love you, you can #KeriOn.

We all have areas that we want to work on and it is within your right to address your weight, your speech pattern, your appearance (clothing wise), however you deem necessary. Just remember that if you don't like yourself on the inside, changing the outside won't fix it. Period. Love yourself inside and outside.

This week's lesson is to accept who you are, flaws and all.

WEEKLY ASSIGNMENT:

Day 1: List the things you like about your appearance. Go on and do it! You cute!!

Day 2: List the things that you can work on that you want to work on.

Day 3: What things make you feel attractive? Do one of them today.

Day 4: If you allow yourself to feel unattractive, what do you lose?

Day 5: When you embrace your melanin and how fly you are, what do you gain?

Week Twenty Eight

Stay encouraged. There's more to come. Keep your fork.#KeriOn

A friend was trying to comfort me during a very frustrating time during the holidays. She said to me, "Keep your fork." I replied, "Huh?" She told me to look it up.

Well, if you have ever attended a four course meal, each time the wait staff picks up the plates, they reply "keep your fork", and finally you realize that you keep the fork for the dessert, which most assume is the best course. So, I say to you, "Keep your fork" and #KeriOn.

In life, challenges and disappointments come, but keep your fork because there is so much more in store for you. "Keep living" as our elders would say, and you will see all the other things in store for you. Work really hard not to get discouraged in moments of disappointment or discomfort. Keep pushing towards the good, sweet life. At times it may be hard, but that is why focusing on the good to come will push you through any hardships.

This week's lesson involves keeping your fork.

WEEKLY ASSIGNMENT:

Day 1: List those challenges where you need to draw on positivity.

Day 2: List the forks that you have in your life (kids, family, great career, vacations, etc).

Day 3: What things make you feel hopeful? Do one of them today.

Day 4: If you allow disappointments to rule, what do you lose?

Day 5: When you keep your fork, what do you gain?

Week Twenty Nine

In very rare cases, you will see a rainbow that wasn't preceded by a storm. However, in most cases, in order to see a rainbow of promise, a storm has to come. Storms vary in intensity and length, so the strength is just in riding it out and knowing it won't last always #KeriOn. When a storm rages, cover yourself and wait on the rainbow of promise that will come.

There are times when you will walk in the sprinkling rain, run in the showers, and take cover in the storm. You will know what response is most appropriate based upon your situation. However, every time there is a storm, stop and search for the rainbow.

The lesson this week is to find the rainbows after major storms in your life.

WEEKLY ASSIGNMENT:

Day 1: List the last three storms of your life.

Day 2: List the rainbows that resulted from the storms.

Day 3: What things make you feel blessed? Do one of them today.

Day 4: If you just focus on the storm only, what do you lose?

Day 5: When you find the rainbows, what do you gain?

Week Thirty

Every fall the trees show us how to let dead things go. #KeriOn

The hardest lesson in life is learning how to let go. How to let go of people, things, or situations. For those persons who desire closure or who harp on the "why" of craziness, you will find yourself stuck and unable to move. Those things and situations are dead and no longer serve you; let go, and #KeriOn.

I have been in situations where I could not logically figure out why a person acted a certain way or adopted certain behaviors, and I would get stuck in trying to figure out the why. Sometimes there is no why. Crazy is just crazy without reason. Let it go. Sometimes there are relationships or friendships that come to an end, but we don't know how to let go. We give too much credit for "time served" and not for what a person positively contributes to our lives. It is pertinent to learn to walk away, let things go when they are dead and stop trying to resuscitate them. Like the trees turning colors in the fall ,and then the leaves die and fall from the limbs, you have to learn to let dead things go as well.

This week's lesson focuses on letting dead things go.

WEEKLY ASSIGNMENT:

Day 1: List those persons or situations that no longer serve you.

Day 2: List the positive things that you must hold on to.

Day 3: What things make you feel valued? Do one of them today.

Day 4: If you allow dead things to linger, what do you lose?

Day 5: When you let go, what do you gain?

Week Thirty One

If your life seems like a soap opera, somebody in the circle is full of drama. #KeriOn.

Do you ever find yourself always in the midst of he say/she say or some family drama? If so, maybe you are the executive producer in your own soap opera. If your associates are always having drama or lend to the drama, try to quell it and disassociate yourself from them. Ever met someone and every time you talk to them it's like "guess what happened?" And you wonder if anything is ever positive or just normal?

Center yourself and stay clear of drama-filled alliances or relationships. They will drain you and turn you into one of the biggest productions ever! Say "No thank you", and #KeriOn.

This week's lesson focuses on aligning yourself with positive things only.

WEEKLY ASSIGNMENT:

Day 1: List those persons that are always full of drama or issues.

Day 2: List the ways to disassociate yourself from drama.

Day 3: What things make you feel at peace? Do one of them today.

Day 4: If you allow constant drama in your life, what do you lose?

Day 5: When you are at peace, what do you gain?

Week Thirty Two

Reserve your "yes" and protect your peace.
#KeriOn

As much as you may want to help others and be there for every single great thing that is happening, you cannot. You have to reserve your yes for the most important things and for those who reciprocate with their yes to support you. When you say yes to everything, you spoil people and drain yourself. This goes back to self-care and learning to #KeriOn.

A part of protecting your peace is not being all over the place and running your mental and physical self ragged. You cannot be your best self if you are running everywhere trying to do everything for others. Reserve your yes for crucial things and to support those who support you.

This week's lesson focuses on protecting your yes.

WEEKLY ASSIGNMENT:

Day 1: List those times when you should have reserved your yes.

Day 2: List the instances where you feel obligated to say yes.

Day 3: What things make you feel supported? Do one of them today.

Day 4: If you say yes to everything, what do you lose?

Day 5: When you protect your yes, what do you gain?

❧❧❧

Week Thirty Three

Don't just be at the table. Own it, and invite others in to eat. #KeriOn

I read a meme that said 'If you're not at the table, you are on the menu'. I laughed heartily at this statement. I was also amused at the number of people who seemingly believe this. Why must you wait on others to invite you to their table? Why not have your own table and then invite others who can positively contribute?

It is your responsibility- if you are blessed- to genuinely make room for others and invite them to the table. Your responsibility does not mean nepotism or promoting those who do not have the drive or skills to get things done, but you should feel a sense of brotherhood that pushes you to pull your brethren up. When you have ownership, you make the rules and you provide the ways and means for growth and upward projection for everyone.

This week's lesson focuses on owning the table.

WEEKLY ASSIGNMENT:

Day 1: List your marketable talents that could be a business venture.

Day 2: List the positive and talented people who can help you realize your vision.

Day 3: What things make you feel entrepreneurial? Do one of them today.

Day 4: If you allow fear to rule, what do you lose?

Day 5: When you look out for others, what do you gain?

Week Thirty Four

No makeup, surgery, or accolades can fix your brokenness. Your soul needs contouring. #KeriOn

In life, we are the result of our cumulative experiences; however, that is no excuse to be mean, a bully, or hateful. I have met some of the most beautiful, smart, and broken men and women because of things they have experienced in their lives. It is important to recognize when you have allowed past experiences to turn you into a negative being.

Have you ever met a beautiful, accomplished woman who was alone or had very few friends? Ever met a man who totally seems to have it all together, but he is a solo person? It is because life has gotten to them. Even in their prime, nothing is attractive about them because they are so broken. They are broken from a lack of love, broken from hurt, broken from bad experiences, and broken with no hopes for healing. They dress it up in Tom Ford, Hermès, Jacqueline Herrera, and Bespoke, but inside their souls are foul and it taints you to keep their company.

For about a year, I dated what I believed to be the most beautiful man I had ever laid eyes on. He was CLEAN, but he lacked empathy. It was hard for him to feel, to empathize, or to allow himself to let his guard down. I will not say that his soul was foul, but he was ice cold and definitely had endured some serious hurt in his lifetime. You cannot fix anyone but yourself and #KeriOn.

This week's lesson is focused on recognizing your brokenness and fixing it.

WEEKLY ASSIGNMENT:

Day 1: List the areas where you have had bad experiences.

Day 2: List the areas where you recognize your brokenness.

Day 3: What things make you feel whole? Do one of them today.

Day 4: If you allow brokenness to rule, what do you lose?

Day 5: When you forgive yourself and others, what do you gain?

Week Thirty Five

Stop drop and roll doesn't work in hell. #KeriOn

As kids we learn all types of drills in case of emergency, but the one that always sticks out is the fire drill. "Stop, drop, and roll if you catch on fire."

Many times, we like to blame others for the poor choices or bad outcomes that we face, but we have free will. No matter the influence, ultimately your decisions are yours and no one else will get punished but you for making them.

We have experienced and witnessed a lot of things, but in the words of your grandmother, "Just because someone else does it doesn't mean that you have to do it." You must be accountable for all of your choices and deeds, right and wrong. If you are a believer in a heaven or hell, then note that stop, drop, and roll does not work in hell. Your best bet is to live a good life and do right by others so that your karma is always good, and you will live your best life while here on earth.

This week's lesson is focused on accountability.

WEEKLY ASSIGNMENT:

Day 1: List those instances where you made bad choices.

Day 2: List the times when you were accountable for your bad choices.

Day 3: What things make you feel like a good person? Do one of them today.

Day 4: If you allow continuous bad choices to rule, what do you lose?

Day 5: When you take accountability and make wiser choices, what do you gain?

Week Thirty Six

When you say you want to build, but you realize that you are at Home Depot- and he's at Lego Land...#KeriOn

---

Relationships. Relationships are harder than "Chinese algebra" when you don't pay attention and are trying to force your own agenda. Many times, we are so busy flaunting it that we are failing at it. Listen to your partner, understand their needs and recognize when you are not on the same page or even in the same book. Be honest with yourself and #KeriOn.

I've often heard men express that they are in the building stages with a woman that they are interested in, but they are fine with being physical early on. If you are building and there are no rooms, figuratively speaking, where are you laying her down? You see, this is a way of stalling and not committing to what this thing between them really is. This is when you realize that 'building' has different meanings. She is at Home Depot, and he is at Lego Land, they are moving toward two different things. Someone has to be adult enough to recognize what it is, call it out, and #KeriOn.

This week's lesson focuses on how to discern whether you are building a real home versus a toy home.

WEEKLY ASSIGNMENT:

Day 1: List the things out that your love interest states she/he is looking for.

Day 2: List the things that you value most in an intimate relationship.

Day 3: What things make you feel loved? Do one of them today.

Day 4: If you allow love games to rule your life, what do you lose?

Day 5: When you allow real love to come, what do you gain?

Week Thirty Seven

If a person invents something, we give them credit. If we cite someone else's work or idea, we give them credit. Why can't we do that with all things? It is okay to compliment others and give them credit for being amazing human beings. It takes nothing away from you to give credit where it's due.

This week's lesson is focused on being able to celebrate with others and acknowledge them on a job well done.

WEEKLY ASSIGNMENT:

Day 1: List three people you admire and why.

Day 2: List how you will express your appreciation of their contributions to society, community, etc.

Day 3: What things make you feel empowering to others? Do one of them today.

Day 4: If you allow jealousy to rule your life, what do you lose?

Day 5: When you value the contributions of others, what do you gain?

Week Thirty Eight

Every morning upon waking, I say the two words, "Thank you". Each day I start with gratitude for another chance to get it right. I practice daily gratitude as I get dressed, as I drive in to work, and go throughout my day. Some days it is hard for me to get through the day, but I always try and find something to be grateful for, even when my body betrays me. That is the mark of living a joyful life.

Everyone around here is chasing happiness. However, I am seeking joy because it is everlasting. There are so many instances where I could have held on to bitterness, but I chose gratitude and to find the joy in the moments. Being drunk with bitterness is a bad look, and it is easy to find persons who are bitter because they have no joy, and they don't want you to have joy either. Move away from them and #KeriOn. Each day is a gift.

This week's lesson is focused on practicing gratitude and finding joy.

WEEKLY ASSIGNMENT:

Day 1: List those instances where you practice gratitude.

Day 2: List the things that you may be bitter about.

Day 3: What things make you feel joy? Do one of them today.

Day 4: If you allow bitterness to rule your life, what do you lose?

Day 5: When you operate in gratitude, what do you gain?

Week Thirty Nine

Grind & Pray. Bless others along the way.
#KeriOn

If you ask anyone about me, they will tell you that I am always working. Even when I feel tired, I am still at home working on something. I rarely have down time, and I sometimes have to remind myself to practice self-care, but I have dreams. My grind is an integral part of my life just like praying several times a day is.

If you are blessed with the ability to hustle and grind and get things done, don't forget to give back as you rise to the top. I am on my way to being wealthy but at this point, I try and bless others by deed, connections, and service. Ask your higher source- in my case, God- how you should use your talent to bless others and to add to the kingdom. It is my duty to serve others and provide

143

opportunities to them where I am able. This is how I #KeriOn.

This week's lesson is focused on blessing others.

WEEKLY ASSIGNMENT:

Day 1: List the ways that you give back to the community.

Day 2: List the opportunities that you are providing for others.

Day 3: What things make you feel like a blessing to others? Do one of them today.

Day 4: If you allow selfishness to rule your life, what do you lose?

Day 5: When you allow selflessness to rule your life, what do you gain?

Week Forty

I have the tendency to be one way at work and another way in my personal life. Balance is important. I am very career-oriented and driven, but that is with a heart towards the communities that I serve in my daily work. I "go hard" for them. God's grace allows me to work in a field that I love and that gives me fulfillment, and I know this is my calling.

I charge you to work in your passion, but with balance. The boss that you are at work should not show up in the home and create chaos or disorder. The tough decision maker and negotiator should not act as if their significant other is the opposing side that needs convincing or muscling. On the other hand, your mother and loving wife side has no place in the work place when negotiating deals. Know when and how to turn things off and on in the appropriate places so that you don't lose your home or your job.

This week's lesson is focused on learning balance.

WEEKLY ASSIGNMENT:

Day 1: List how you "show up" at work.

Day 2: List how you "show up" at home.

Day 3: What things make you feel balanced? Do one of them today.

Day 4: If you allow the boss to rule your home, what do you lose?

Day 5: When you allow balance in your life, what do you gain?

Week Forty One

If you describe your relationship as off/ on....when y'all are off, who is he on? #KeriOn

I met a great guy and he described his relationship status as off and on for over a year. Well, whether or not that was true, I was surprised that he was cool with the limbo status of his relationship and was using it to his advantage to not appear attached. But with the rampant increase in HIV, STDs, and domestic violence, it is best to be sure about people's relationship status.

The greater question is, when y'all are off, who is your significant other on? You cannot trust your health in the hands of others. It is 100% YOUR responsibility to have the conversations about trust, your body, sexual habits, and disease status and still use protection. There is no blaming the other person because YOU didn't protect yourself. If you can talk politics, celebrity gossip, literature or sports, then you can talk sexual health.

This week's lesson is focused on having the conversations about safer sex.

WEEKLY ASSIGNMENT:

Day 1: List the questions you should ask any potential sexual partner.

Day 2: List the types of tests that you will require a partner to show you or take with you.

Day 3: What things make you feel empowered with your health? Do one of them today.

Day 4: If you allow lust and undefined relationships to rule your life, what do you lose?

Day 5: When you protect yourself in all aspects, what do you gain?

Week Forty Two

We teach best what we most need to learn.

#KeriOn

What lesson do you keep repeating in your life? Think about it and think on how you can help others like you to learn that lesson. We teach best what we need to learn...think about it. You are your own best case study.

I can teach about stress and coping because I am always learning new coping methods to deal with stress regardless of the stressor. Coping comes in various forms, and I embrace the majority of those that are out there that are not chemically induced. I have to address my stressors to protect my overall health and stay in a state of relaxation to keep from getting sick.

This week's lesson is focused on recognizing your stressors and coping strategies.

WEEKLY ASSIGNMENT:

Day 1: List the things that stress you out and how you cope.

Day 2: List the ways that you can teach others how to excel.

Day 3: What things make you feel helpful? Do one of them today.

Day 4: If you allow stress to rule your life, what do you lose?

Day 5: When you teach others what you do, what do you gain?

Week Forty Three

What people think about you is none of your business. #KeriOn

---

This lesson is the simplest of them all. What other people think about you is not your concern. Do not occupy yourself with the why or the how, and if anyone brings you additional information about what others think of you, be wary of them as well. Focus on your purpose, what you think of yourself, and what your Creator thinks of you.

This week's lesson focuses on valuing self.

WEEKLY ASSIGNMENT:

Day 1: List how you view yourself.

Day 2: List how you want to be viewed by the Creator.

Day 3: What things make you feel valued and purposeful? Do one of them today.

Day 4: If you allow what others think of you to rule your life, what do you lose?

Day 5: When you value yourself above what others think, what do you gain?

❧

Week Forty-Four

If someone has accomplished something that you once desired, nobody really wants to hear the story of how you almost or you could've. #KeriOn

I am always encouraging people to pursue their dreams. If your dream involves higher education, running a major company, owning your own company or joining a Black Greek Letter Organization, go for it! But please remember that although others know that you are networking or interested in a similar path, not one person wants to hear your story about how you were almost a Kappa, or how you really wanted to go into medicine but chose business. It is like you're at your 25th reunion, and the high school football player who lives in his glory days is talking about how he almost went to Auburn and played for their team.

With the exception of going back to play college ball, you still have time to achieve your dreams. There is more than enough opportunity to become whoever you dreamt you would be at this stage. Go forth and #KeriOn.

This lesson focuses on how to get back to your dreams.

WEEKLY ASSIGNMENT:

Day 1: List your career and social goals (at least three).

Day 2: List how you can reach each of the goals that you set.

Day 3: What things make you feel fulfilled? Do one of them today.

Day 4: If you allow unfulfilled dreams to rule your life, what do you lose?

Day 5: When you work towards your goals, what do you gain?

Week Forty Five

*When the past comes knocking, act like there
is no door. It's only selling dreams. Those are
already free. #KeriOn*

"Hey, big head." That phrase is familiar around birthdays, holidays, and when exes are lonely. Why do we entertain these people? They are exes for a reason. It didn't work out, so hasn't everyone decided to #KeriOn? In some cases, you are missed, and a person is apologetic; however, you are not obligated to open any doors or take back anyone who didn't value you.

Stand your ground on the decision you made and don't allow others to vacillate in and out of your life. A pattern of inconsistent people creates comfortability and sends the wrong messages. Your future is ahead of you, and the past is behind you. When it comes knocking, draw the curtains, turn off all of the lights, and pretend you are not home. A person must prove that they have truly changed and learned their lesson so that you are not used and abused for a second time. You deserve love and care and most importantly, respect. The more you allow vacillation, the less respect they have for you.

This week's lesson is focused on closing the door, locking it and pretending to change your address.

WEEKLY ASSIGNMENT:

Day 1: List the people in your past who still contact you.

Day 2: List why you think that you NEED them in your life.

Day 3: What things do these people do to make you feel valued? Do one of them together today.

Day 4: If you allow everyone to vacillate in and out of your life, what do you lose?

Day 5: When you decided there's no future in your past, what do you gain?

Week Forty Six

No man has ever loved you enough to stay. Don't
be a placeholder or practice wife. #KeriOn

This is for all persons. Men, just replace the nouns with your choice of noun. If you have ever been a serial monogamist, you will get what I am saying. You are always in a relationship, but never the chosen one to carry his name- perhaps his seed, but not his name. I know, that stings. While I understand that marriage should never be a goal or an endgame, there are many who are practice wives/husbands.

Seat-fillers are used to make the room look full- just like practice spouses are used to make people's lives look full and fulfilling. The person who loves you or claims to have deep feelings for you is always around reaping all of the benefits of a spouse- attending your company outings, doing holidays with the family, but never commits, and as soon as you break up, they get married - to someone else!! You, my dear, are a practice spouse. People keep practicing with you, but don't actually make you a spouse-cut it out! It is within your power. Stop the behavior by ending all of the extras and doing the most.

This week's lesson focuses on taking your power back in relationships.

WEEKLY ASSIGNMENT:

Day 1: List your last three failed relationships and how you treated them.

Day 2: List when you noticed their behavior changing - is there a pattern?

Day 3: What things make you feel loved by your significant other? Do it for yourself today.

Day 4: If you allow others to keep practicing with you, what do you lose?

Day 5: When you value yourself enough to quit doing wife things for boyfriends, what do you gain?

Week Forty Seven

There is NO shame in surviving. Those who cannot comprehend are often lying about their own survival. Don't own other people's stuff. #KeriOn

I am often questioned about my resilience, my ability to move on in grace, and have the life that I have after enduring some pretty terrible things. I say it's not me, it's God. I have no idea where my resilience came from; it is truly inherent. If I ever allow myself to really "go there" and think about it all, it can be overwhelming. But there is no shame in my surviving, or yours.

I find that people will say things like, "Oh that couldn't have been me". Let me be clear. You have NO idea how you will react until a thing actually happens to you. And Lord knows, I have had enough happenings to be my own case study for that finding. I will receive all kinds of questions and judgments regarding the how, the why, etc. and people pretend not to be able to comprehend, but live in families with all kinds of secrets about survival. Those who don't recognize their own emotional abuse is just as damaging as sexual or physical abuse. I say to all survivors, don't own other people's stuff and feel the need to validate your experience against their ignorance.

This week's lesson is about owning your own story without shame or guilt.

WEEKLY ASSIGNMENT:

Day 1: List the things you are proud you survived.

Day 2: List how you healed from the things you survived - keep these strategies nearby.

Day 3: What things make you feel empowered? Do one of them today.

Day 4: If you allow victimization to rule your life, what do you lose?

Day 5: When you stand in your power and truth, what do you gain?

⸙

Week Forty Eight

It's the BUT in our lives that make us beautiful, complex beings. #KeriOn

But is a word that signifies what you stated before has pivoted. Have you ever seen a ballerina or a gymnast pivot? It is a beautiful thing. I find the "but"- the pivot, synonymous with the semi-colon- life goes on, and it can be beautiful. What if you lived the first half of your life exactly as your parents planned it -'BUT'- you decided that you were not happy and decided to #KeriOn?

Sometimes in life, we do everything as we are told and operate in a mechanical fashion. We used to work at jobs for 25-30 years before retiring- but not anymore. Professionals all used to look like the librarian or the preacher- but not anymore. Family values and discipline used to be the center of community morals- but not anymore. It's the 'buts' that now make us unpredictable and different; it makes us beautiful, complex beings that cannot be boxed into categories. Be you. Be all of you without apology.

This week's lesson focuses on naming your beautiful complex nature.

WEEKLY ASSIGNMENT:

Day 1: Write out a short bio about you- not what you have accomplished, but about you.

Day 2: List how you created your "buts" at certain stages of life.

Day 3: What things make you feel beautiful? Do one of them today.

Day 4: If you allow what others to dictate who you are, what do you lose?

Day 5: When you value your "but", what do you gain?

Week Forty Nine

Desire versus Desperation. #KeriOn

We are in a time when Black women are a definite market for "how to get married" and fix yourself solely to catch a king. I think we as women of color should be clear that some of us- not all- desire to be married but aren't desperate. Stop giving people a market for classes to help you when your Granny didn't need any help and neither did your Mom.

To catch a king is what it seems to be all about. Books, posts, articles, tv shows, and music all cater to the thought that somehow we are unwanted for life but good enough for sex. Don't sell yourself short! Make your desire known so that you are building with real wood and not Legos, and don't settle. But also don't allow yourself to be mistreated out of desperation. Somehow, someway the message of desperation has crept in and we need to change the narrative, Sis.

This week's lesson focuses on you being enough.

WEEKLY ASSIGNMENT:

Day 1: List how you know that you are enough.

Day 2: List the ways in which you can meet a quality mate and engage in healthy behaviors.

Day 3: What things make you feel desired? Do one of them today.

Day 4: If you allow desperation to rule your life, what do you lose?

Day 5: When you make your desire known, what do you gain?

Week Fifty

No one can tell me what I am worth. No one but God will dictate my story. He is the author and finisher of my story, period. Embrace who you are, where you are from, and your truth. When I tell people that I am from Decatur, I am proud. There is no shame in where I am from or circumstances surrounding where I grew up. Many of us are proud and have accomplished great things in our lives.

I walk in my truth and before anyone can tell you about me, I will tell you about me. I do not live outside of my story and listen to others narrate as they will. My life and my work speak for themselves. How is your story told?

No one can narrate it or navigate it better than you can. Be the co-author with God to finish your story how you see fit and to own it without shame. Hold your head high, and #KeriOn.

WEEKLY ASSIGNMENT:

Day 1: List the most important elements of your story.

Day 2: List the most disturbing elements of your story - own them.

Day 3: What positive things make you feel courageous? Do one of them today.

Day 4: If you allow others to tell your story, what do you lose?

Day 5: When you tell your own story, what do you gain?

Week Fifty One

Be you and only you because on your best day, you could never be me, nor I you. #KeriOn

Figuratively speaking, I have worn heels, steel toe boots, Timbs and walked bare feet across hot coals in my lifetime, and no one can do my life better than me. I can never imagine enduring all that you have and still standing by grace because that is not my story, it is yours. You were meant to live to #KeriOn.

Role models are all well and good, but make them realistic. Be your authentic self- with blends of Beyoncé. I was confused seeing grown women (over 40) idolizing her because my values are different from what they were praising. Do I believe that she is an amazing entertainer, marketing guru, woke Mother, and great business woman? Absolutely. But I have no desire to be her or model myself after her. On her best day, she could never be me. Yep, I said it. I'm not talking about looks or material possessions. I am talking about walking in other people's shoes from start to finish. On my best day I could never be her, either. That's the beauty of her being Beyoncé and me being me. I feel the same way about Oprah, Shonda Rhimes, and others that I admire, but don't aspire to be. I am meant to be me in all of my greatness, however local that may be, or if I am only family famous, I am content.

This week's lesson focuses on living your best life.

WEEKLY ASSIGNMENT:

Day 1: List how you view yourself.

Day 2: List your most grandiose ideal self.

Day 3: What things make you feel authentic? Do one of them today.

Day 4: If you allow comparisons to rule your life, what do you lose?

Day 5: When you value yourself as you are with your appointed gifts, what do you gain?

Week Fifty Two

Distractions will keep you from the promise.
FOCUS. #KeriOn

In life, we oftentimes are faced with opportunities to grow that may be painful. There is so much purpose in this pain and we have to stay the course in order to grow and move to the next level that will propel us to greater heights. During these times of change, where we are faced with our most important decisions, we become distracted by people, situations, and oppositions that aren't new.

Have you ever asked yourself, "Why does this person keep appearing in my life?" It is because you have failed the test time and time again of learning to push past problems and focusing on the outcome to be able to make it to a better space or place. An ex, a problem family member, or a challenging co-worker - all of these are distractions from your purpose. Once you recognize this, you are then empowered to ignore, focus, and #KeriOn. Pass the test to get to what is promised to you and what is exclusively meant for you. Learn to get "unstuck" and stop focusing on them. They are deliberate distractions for a reason. Problem family members cannot be healed by your efforts or attention. That ex is an ex for a reason and hasn't changed. The challenging co-worker desires to keep you from reaching greater heights and is purposely there to distract you.

This week, your challenge is to list out those persons or situations that always "knock you off your game" so that you easily recognize the distractions when they come. If you name a thing and give a face to it, then you recognize and can address it accordingly when faced with it again. Think of the things that keep you in good spirits, laughing, smiling, and upbeat… surround yourself with those things. Again, give NO energy to the person or situation that is negative. Do you need to say the words to anyone, like you are a distraction? No. What is understood does not need to be explained. All you need to do is STOP participating and simply #KeriOn.

WEEKLY ASSIGNMENT:

Day 1: List those persons and situations that distract you.

Day 2: List the current opportunities that you have in front of you.

Day 3: What positive things help you to focus on your goals? Do one of them today.

Day 4: If you allow distractions to win, what do you lose?

Day 5: When you focus, what do you gain?

Sources

Murakami, Haruki. 2007. What I Talk About When I Talk About Running. Knopf Publishing.

Thomas, Roger Williams. 1996. A 3rd Serving of Chicken Soup for the Soul. *Keep Your Fork*.